Dear Parent:
Your child's love of reading

Every child learns to read in a different way and at his or her own speed. You can help your young reader improve and become more confident by encouraging his or her own interests and abilities. You can also guide your child's spiritual development by reading stories with biblical values and Bible stories, like I Can Read! books published by Zonderkidz. From books your child reads with you to the first books he or she reads alone, there are I Can Read! books for every stage of reading:

SHARED READING
Basic language, word repetition, and whimsical illustrations, ideal for sharing with your emergent reader.

BEGINNING READING
Short sentences, familiar words, and simple concepts for children eager to read on their own.

READING WITH HELP
Engaging stories, longer sentences, and language play for developing readers.

READING ALONE
Complex plots, challenging vocabulary, and high-interest topics for the independent reader.

ADVANCED READING
Short paragraphs, chapters, and exciting themes for the perfect bridge to chapter books.

I Can Read! books have introduced children to the joy of reading since 1957. Featuring award-winning authors and illustrators and a fabulous cast of beloved characters, I Can Read! books set the standard for beginning readers.

A lifetime of discovery begins with the magical words **"I Can Read!"**

Visit www.icanread.com for information on enriching your child's reading experience.
Visit www.zonderkidz.com for more Zonderkidz I Can Read! titles.

With my great power and outstretched arm I made the earth
and its people and the animals that are on it, and I give it to
anyone I please.

—*Jeremiah 27:5*

ZONDERKIDZ

Polar Pals
Copyright © 2011 by Zonderkidz

Requests for information should be addressed to:
Zonderkidz, *Grand Rapids, Michigan* 49530

Library of Congress Cataloging-in-Publication Data

Polar pals.
     p. cm.
  ISBN 978-0-310-72188-8 (softcover)
  1. Animals—Religious aspects—Christianity—Juvenile literature. 2. Animals—Arctic regions—
Juvenile literature. 3. Creation—Juvenile literature.
  BT746.P66 2011
  231.7—dc22   2010039463

Editor: Mary Hassinger
Art direction: Jody Langley

Printed in China
11 12 13 14 15 16 17 /SCC/ 10 9 8 7 6 5 4 3 2 1

MADE·BY·GOD

Polar Pals

CONTENTS

God made many animals.

Some live where it is warm,

like the roadrunner.

Some live where it is very cold,

like the …

EMPEROR PENGUIN!

The emperor penguin lives

in Antarctica near the South Pole.

Sometimes it can be 42 degrees F below zero!

The water where they

swim and catch food

might be only 28 degrees F!

That is colder than ice.

The emperor penguin is the
biggest penguin—they
can be four feet tall.
They might weigh 65 pounds.

These penguins cannot fly.

God made sure they are great swimmers

since they spend most of their

lives in the sea

looking for food like

krill and squid.

Emperor penguins live in huge colonies.

While the father penguins take care of their babies, the colony works to keep everyone warm by staying close together.

Another kind of cold-weather bird that stays together is the …

ARCTIC TERN!

The arctic tern is a small bird that
lives in large groups
called colonies, just like penguins.

The tern can be 12 inches long

and weigh two to four ounces.

They eat mostly small fish

they catch by diving down

to the water.

Many birds fly south for the winter.
The arctic tern has the longest
trip of any bird.
They breed in the Arctic tundra—
the North Pole—and then fly
to the edge of Antarctica for the
winter.
That is over 21,750 miles—
almost as many miles as the
circumference of the earth!

These special cold-weather birds

travel with their colonies.

Right before they take off,

the whole colony gets

very, very quiet … that is

called "dread."

Then, all of a sudden, they

all take off together.

Another animal that loves the cold
is the …

POLAR BEAR!

Polar bears live in the Arctic.

They can be found in areas of Alaska,

Canada, Greenland, Norway,

and Russia.

They spend most of their
lives in the sea hunting for
seal, walruses, and other small
water animals.
Polar bears do not drink water.

Father polar bears are called boars.

Mothers are called sows.

They can grow to be ten feet long

and weigh 1,700 pounds!

When a mother bear has cubs,

she usually has twins.

She builds a snow den and sleeps

all winter, waiting for her babies.

The father is active all year long.

God gave polar bears two layers
of fur.

One layer is thick and woolly.

It is close to the skin and keeps
the bear warm.

They also have hollow guard hairs.
These stick up and protect the bear
from getting wet.
These hairs are like clear straws
(not white).
The white-looking coat camouflages
polar bears in the snow and ice.

Another Arctic animal that
God gave great camouflage to
is the …

ARCTIC FOX!

This special fox is found
farther north than any other
land mammal in the world.

Their fur is white in the winter
and turns gray-brown in
the summertime.
This is helpful if they want
to hide and also when they hunt.

A male fox is called a reynard.

A mother fox is called a vixen,

and her babies are kits.

God gave the foxes a big,

bushy tail.

One way they use their tail

is to keep warm.

When they go to sleep they

tuck it around their feet and nose.

It also helps them change direction

when they are running.

God is so good!

He makes sure that all of his

creatures have what they need

to live in the hot as well as

the very cold parts of the world.